CHANGE OUR SCHOOLS THROUGH PRAYER

A 10-DAY DEVOTIONAL FOR SCHOOL LEADERS

SUZANNE WEATHERS

MLSTIMPSON ENTERPRISES

Copyright © 2019 by Suzanne Weathers

Published by MLStimpson Enterprises

P.O. Box 1592

Cedar Hill, TX 75106-1592

ISBN: 978-1-943563-24-1

All rights reserved.

No part of this book may be reproduced in any form or by any electronic or mechanical means, including information storage and retrieval systems, without written permission from the author, except for the use of brief quotations in a book review.

CONTENTS

Acknowledgments	v
Introduction	ix
1. Power and Authority	1
2. Region and Territory	9
3. The School – Elementary, Middle, and High School	15
4. The School Building	21
5. Our Families	25
6. The Teachers and Support Staff	29
7. The Community	33
8. The Operations	37
9. The Organization	43
10. The Educational System	47
About the Author	51

ACKNOWLEDGMENTS

When asked by the Holy Spirit to write this devotional book, my first reaction was, WHAT? I am not a writer by any means. Then I heard that still, soft voice say, *But you are an intercessor and you pray for your school every day.* This was true, but I never thought to share those prayers with anyone else but God. I guess I was wrong.

The first time I heard anything about writing a book was from a lady that spoke a prophetic word to me during a Tuesday night prayer meeting at my church. She said, "I see you writing articles and books." I didn't know how to receive it, so I didn't. I realized now that was the Lord sending me a 'hint' months before the assignment was given. Thank you to that unknown prayer warrior who heard from the Lord and spoke His words to me.

I want to thank Pastor April Barker, Dream Builder for Empire of Dream LLC. Before I ever wrote a word on a piece of paper I came to her with the mandate from the

Holy Spirit and the title the Lord gave me and she worked with me to make this dream a reality. Thank you, Pastor April, for enduring all my endless texts of insecurity and doubt about whether I could even do this or not. You always had a word of encouragement and pointed me back on the path. I could not have completed this assignment without your guidance and support. Thank you.

I have to give a special shout out to my daughter, Lydia, who from the moment she heard that I was writing a book would say, "Go Mom and write that New York Times Best Seller book!" She has been the voice inside my head throughout this whole process. She caught on to the vision and saw its success before I had written a word. I am so grateful to her for believing in me and pushing me it.

I don't think I could have done any of this without the love of my life, my husband, Michael. I have to say thank you to him for putting up with me at four in the morning writing chapters on my cell phone. I know that light was a bug, but you were a trooper through it all. Thank you for loving me through this process and believing that I could make it through.

Thank you for my friends and family members that shared in this journey with me. Your prayers and words of encouragement were truly the "wind beneath my wings."

DEDICATION

My Husband – my biggest fan and a great educator.
For Leah, Lydia, Lauren, and Liberty – my homeschool.
Pastor Jim and Becky Henessey - spiritual covering.
Mr. Fincher, Roxanne Ashley, Sharon Duplantier, Kristen Algier,
Priscilla Parhms, and Kristina Nanini – my teachers.
Every school leader.

Not by might,
Nor by power,
But by My Spirit saith the Lord of hosts.
Zechariah 4:6b KJV

INTRODUCTION

"and My people, who are called by My Name, humble themselves, and pray and seek (crave, require as a necessity) My face and turn from their wicked ways, then I will hear [them] from heaven, and forgive their sin and heal their land." 2 Chronicles 7:14 AMP

"But you are A CHOSEN RACE, A royal PRIESTHOOD, A CONSECRATED NATION, A [special] PEOPLE FOR God's OWN POSSESSION, so that you may proclaim the excellencies [the wonderful deeds and virtues and perfections] of Him who called you out of darkness into His marvelous light." 1 Peter 2:9 AMP

Being a principal is a call, so much more than it is a career. God has to place a unique burden on your heart to steward His children and families in the educational realm. I didn't realize that at the time of my "calling" into this work.

x | INTRODUCTION

I was a 6th grade middle school teacher when a gift of leadership began to emerge. I was always a teacher with great classroom management. My kids both loved and feared me; it was the perfect combination. I didn't know then that was the anointing of a Heavenly Father within my classroom. It was a safe place for scholars to be themselves and develop inquiry based learning, but also a place where parents could laugh, love, cry, and advocate for what was best for their child. My classroom was safe. But I knew even then this burden was so much bigger than the four walls my classroom could contain.

I knew it was a calling of impact that would not only change the scholars in my class, but those within the school. I began to have teachers come to me and ask about my management style and how I maintained engagement at the same time. I began to coach and support them. My classroom management style was becoming infectious. I could feel a tide was turned and I could hear the "call" far off.

Defining Moment

One day, my Director at the time asked me to be in charge of the middle school for two days, while the administrative staff were at a leadership training off campus. I had never had this experience before, but my Director was confident that I was ready. For those two days, I was the acting administrator for the middle school. I had a group of friends, I called them WWIMC (Wonderful Women In My

Circle), and they were my prayer partners for years on that campus.

For those two days, they would meet with me in the morning before I started the day of leadership and pray, and then at the end of the school day, we would meet again and thank God for His strength and presence on the campus. During those two days I was in charge, the school ran smoothly. There were little to no incidents, and I was able to support teachers when needed and walk hallways praying during periods.

My very presence seemed to shift the atmosphere. During passing periods, where there usually seemed to be chaos and mayhem, with me in the hallways, literally waiting for them, the scholars transitioned to class without the confusion we have had in the past. At the end of those two days, the school was operating at a higher level of order and respect. Teachers were less stressed because of the direct support I was able to give them and scholars felt safe having my presence in the hallways and after school. You could feel the spirit of the Lord in that school on those two days.

Well, at the end of my brief stint as acting administrator, my prayer friends laid hands on me and prayed my regained strength as I headed back into the classroom the next week. We praised God for the peace He brought to the building and His weighty presence inside every scholar and every staff member. It was only God, and we gave Him all the glory and praise.

At the end of that week, we had a team Agape circle.

During the Agape circle, teachers around the circle began to talk about how supported and safe they felt when I was in charge. How the school had a different feel and the scholars were on their best behavior knowing I was around. There was so much love in the room and somehow I knew this was significant.

The director made an announcement to everyone in the circle and said, "Suzanne, you are a leader. If you ever wondered who you are or what you should be doing, you are a leader and you should be leading." At that very moment the room grew silent and all eyes were on me, not in judgment, but in quiet agreement. I knew at that moment something had shifted for me. The chapter of 'Suzanne the classroom teacher' had come to a close, and a new chapter was emerging...the Call to leadership.

The call to write this book came from a class I was attending at my church called Pubic School Impact. In the first class I attended, there were about a half dozen to a dozen teachers in attendance and several parents and individuals that had a call to pray for schools and the children in them, but there were only two principals in the room.

I felt like we needed prayer, but we also needed to pray. We needed to pray about this position that we had been commissioned to stand in. The first class was all about how prayer would be the only way that our schools would change, and how we would as a class cover our school districts in prayer.

That consistent theme left me thinking about all the

times when I was a teacher and even as a parent I had spent in my prayer closet, praying for my schools and those in charge. Prayer gave me the courage to send my kids to schools and entrust them to complete strangers; prayer gave me the wisdom and knowledge to be able to teach those same children and instill trust in their parents that I was there for them and their children, to give them the best education I could. And I found myself in the same place of prayer and supplication as I walked into this chapter of leadership.

I knew that I would need the Holy Spirit's discernment and His anointing to be able to see the vision that the Lord wanted to execute not only within the school that I was assigned to, but for the network that my leadership would impact. The more I sat at that first meeting, the stronger the feeling of the only thing that could make a change in the educational system was the power of prayer. And not just the prayers of the parents and teachers, but it was going to have to be the prayers of the principal to begin to steer this ship in the right direction.

That first meeting ended in prayer, and I heard the Holy Spirit say to me, *You need to write the book, "Change Our Schools through Prayer".*

I immediately rejected the idea. I talked myself out of all of the reasons why I didn't have the time nor the talent to do what the Lord was asking me to do. Isn't that ironic? Who was I to tell the Lord that He must have this all wrong? I wasn't the right person for this mission.

Yet, I could not get away from the tugging in my heart

that it need to be written. Written to and for all the many principals that need to exercise their power and authority over their Godly assignments. No longer can we sit by as passive participants in a system that is making and molding our next generation of leaders. We have to stand up, in the spirit, and began to degree and declare what the Lord wants to happen in our schools and began to align that vision with the prayers of the parents and teachers.

When it comes to prayer there is no time to start like the present. Please join me on this prayer journey by accepting the call to pray for the next ten days over your school community and those who have been called to lead.

∽

Dear Father,

We hear Your clarion call in this hour for Your leaders to arise out of their slumber. You are calling us to look up and see Your vision for this educational system. We say YES to Your call in our lives. We will fall on our knees and take our petition unto You. No longer will we resist the call or fall into the world system of leadership.

We will follow You as Christ followed You, Father. We are sorry for the times we ignored the pushes in our spirit to stop and pray for our schools, teachers, students, and parents and we chose to turn to evil and complain when the change was in the power of our confessions and declaration to You. Father, thank You for continuing to call our name and choosing us to represent You in our schools across the nation. It's no light task, but we are ready and willing to dive deeper with You. Father, we love You and are so humbled and honored to be Your servant leaders in this time of shifting. Change educational systems through me this day. I am here Lord, send me. In Jesus' Matchless Name, Amen.

POWER AND AUTHORITY

"They were all astonished *and* in awe, and *began* saying to one another, 'What is this message? For with authority and power He commands the unclean spirits and they come out!'" Luke 4:36 AMP

"After that comes the end (completion), when He hands over the kingdom to God the Father, after He has made inoperative *and* abolished every ruler and every authority and power." I Corinthians 15:24 AMP

"and to have authority *and* power to cast out demons." Mark 3:15 AMP

Many teachers seek to go into leadership because they think power and authority comes from a position or title that you hold. They have great ideas and a voice that can change the very atmosphere of a school building. I was that kind of educator.

I was a leader before it was ever announced at that Agape Circle that day. I was leading my school from my classroom. The effect that my leadership call would have on the scholars that I would teach every year and the teacher I would mentor and the teams I would guide and support confirmed that I was moving in the right direction on my school leadership journey

At the time, I didn't notice that the place of power and authority was not so much in the classroom, but it was what I did, faithfully, before I came into the school. It was my secret place of prayer.

In the educational world, teachers need to develop as classroom management or behavior management, but the spiritual mantle that they would need to operate in is God's gift of power and authority. There is such spiritual warfare that happens within a school and in the classroom. It's so important that those in charge exercise the power and authority that Christ gave His believers within our schools and with our students. When I was praying about stepping into this principal position, I was searching for what I could bring to a school that would bring about change and impact. A friend of mine said, "You have a gift of order. When you come into a place, whether it is a classroom or a school, your presence brings things into order." As I began to mediate on those words, I looked back at my first two-day leadership assignment.

I was so nervous. I didn't know what God and the network were thinking to put me in charge of a school of 525 scholars and 34 staff members. I was so overwhelmed by the assignment I actually hid in my office, overcome with fear.

I had the Chief Academic Officer come and visit the campus, and he said something that I would never forget. He said, "You have to get out of this office and get on the floor. Half of the things that are happening wouldn't if you were out there so they can see you. Your presence changes everything." What I heard in the spirit is, *If you don't get out there in that school, I can't be out there, Suzanne. For the power and authority that I have given you is for this school. Everything and everyone in this building is subject to My spirit, to My power and authority. And as you walk these hallways and visit these classroom, you allow My spirit to permeate the atmosphere and establish Kingdom rulership.*

I had no choice. I had to get out there and exercise the leadership weapons of power and authority to bring Godly order in the school I was assigned to.

As I began to step out more into the hallways during passing periods or into classrooms as the teacher was teaching, my very presence changed the atmosphere. Scholars would straighten up and pay closer attention, and teachers would teach with more boldness and confidence because divine alignment had been established by my presence. God's word said, "Behold, I give unto you power to tread on serpents and scorpions, and over all the power of the enemy: and nothing shall by any means hurt you." Luke 10:19 KJV

Principals, that's the power and authority that lies within you. You don't have to let violence, crime, and destruction be a part of your campus. You carry the power and authority to tell those things to GO! And they have to because of the greater one that lives inside of you.

Don't be deceived; it's not the title or the position that gives you access to those weapons. It's your relationship with God and Him standing up BIG in you. God has called you to be the 'gatekeepers' of your schools. It is you who will stand on the wall and hear what the Lord has to say about the students and their families. It is up to us to pray from heaven's perspective and allow God's will to be done on earth as it has already been decreed and declared from heaven.

When you are positioned in a place of power and authority, your prayer language changes. You are no longer asking the Lord to intervene on your school's behalf, but you are speaking the things that the spirit of God is revealing to you about the school, and you declaring them to be so. You now stand, not only in the position of power, but under the authority of the Lordship of Jesus Christ. You are His ambassador and you now represent Him in that school.

As I am writing this, I can remember what my principal coach would say to me when I first started this journey. "What do you see for your school? What does it sound like, look like, feel like to you?"

Those questions were so frustrating to me in the beginning, because I didn't see anything. I was trying to build a vision from within myself instead of tapping into the vision that God had for that school and to speak that with power and authority. Once I started to ask the Lord the same questions that my coach was asking me, and stopped and listened, I could see the school through the eyes of the spirit. I could hear what God wanted this school to represent to families and the community. And that's where I needed to stand. This spiritual revelation has changed the way I lead and the way I follow leaders.

I began to understand that there is a place of power and authority that requires me to do something. I must walk out the call that had been placed on my life. I have to dream, I have to listen, and then I must move. We all must move in the authority given to us.

This is something that we cannot do by ourselves, but only by the hand of the Lord can this power and authority make the needed impact in our schools. Let's pray that the Lord will give us vision for the schools that we have been assigned to and the boldness to speak forth what He has shown us in power and authority.

∽

Heavenly Father,

As we begin to activate our call into the educational system, Lord, give us the boldness to use the weapons that You have equipped us with in this hour. You said in Your word that all power and authority has been given us, so Lord, teach us every day how to walk in that mantle. Let us wear it in confidence knowing that we are praying to You from heaven down.

Download Your plans for our schools, our students, our teachers, and our families, so, that we may decree a thing and it shall come to pass. Our schools will be changed, our students will be changed, our teachers will be changed, our communities will be changed all because we took our place as gatekeepers on the wall of the educational system.

Father, You said whatsoever You bind in earth shall be bound in heaven, so Father we bind every plot and plan of the enemy to steal, kill, and destroy our schools and classrooms in the name of Jesus. No longer will our students be victims to premature death, depression, destruction, and soul decay. Father, we loose Your abundant life into every student and faculty member in my school. No weapon formed against them shall be able to prosper, and any tongue that rises up against them shall be condemned.

We say No! Not on our watch!

We will speak life in their homes, with their friends, in their classes, with their teachers. Life!

Father, You said in Your word that we have the power and authority to tread upon serpents and nothing by any means shall harm us. Father, let us not be concerned about harm coming to us as principals, but let us step out in faith, knowing You are our *shield and buckler and You are our rearguard. Father, thank You for these weapons and this new mantle as we walk daily in the assignment You have given us. We are humbled and full of gratitude. In Jesus' Name we pray. Amen.*

REGION AND TERRITORY

"And You have not given me into the hand of the enemy; You have set my feet in a broad place."
Psalms 31:8 AMP

"I have given you every place on which the sole of your foot treads, just as I promised to Moses." Joshua 1:3 AMP

In the short time that I have been in school leadership, I have been assigned into three areas: Southwest Dallas, West Dallas, and Grand Prairie. In each of those areas, I believe God uniquely designed for me to be there and to make an impact. As I looked back at each of them, and even in the one I am in right now, I believe my assignment was fulfilled. When I first started in Southwest Dallas, I thought, *This would be the school I will start and end my career at.*

I had been a teacher in that same campus for over five years and I was truly the "people's choice" for principal. I was very comfortable at that school and in that area and territory because they were people I lived next to and could relate to. The school was 85-90 percent African American and so was the staff at that time. This was the place I was sure I belonged. And for that year, I do believe that territory was my assignment. I would faithfully arrive to work early, before any of the teachers would arrive, just to walk the building and speak life over the staff and their scholars.

I felt that weight of my assignment to the school was not just for the scholars, parents, and teachers, it was for the community. God has placed a mandate in my heart to love and cover the whole community in prayer. This assignment came easily because it was my hometown. I felt a vested interest in the people, the businesses that partnered with the school, and the outside agencies that would provide services to our scholars. I knew that I needed God's wisdom and knowledge to bring the right people into this school to speak a word of encouragement and hope.

There was a rumor in the neighborhood that because the school was predominately an African American population—both staff and students alike—that it was low in academics and high in behavior problems. This narrative had begun to penetrate itself into the very hallways of our school and change the atmosphere. I believe I was sent there to revitalize hope and let them know that what people were saying about them did not have to be their truth. I began to pray God's truth every morning around that building—in and outside, speaking to the very land and atmosphere around that school to change. I asked God to blow a fresh new perspective for that school into the hearts and minds of the community they served. As we were faithful to praying over the school, we began to see a decrease in our behavioral referrals, a peace and patience emerge out of our teachers, stronger relationships with families in the community, and increased academic growth. We began to feel the wind of change and hope in our hallways now, and rumors were no longer centered around all that was going wrong in the school, but all that was going right for our students.

When my assignment there was over, the Lord directed me to West Dallas. The needs of this school were directly impacted by the community in which it was located. The community itself and school district did not want a charter school in their community. They believed that the charter school would take away from the public school and erode the community. At this time and for several years prior, the schools in that area code were one of the lowest performing areas in local independent school district in both reading and math. There was a need for a higher standards for the students and the community.

This assignment was very different for me. I was not familiar with this community at all. The population was predominately Hispanic, but the staff did not reflect the population they served. So, there was a challenge in bridging the gap with families and the community as a whole. Little did I know, that was my assignment—to begin to build that bridge. During my two years at this school, I initiated, during the Lent season, a community prayer walk. Every Saturday during the Lenten season, I would go to the school—sometimes alone, sometimes with my daughter, or some people at the school—and walk the neighborhood that surrounded the school and stop at specific locations and pray. It was so impactful. Not only did we believe that God would hear our prayers, but it opened our eyes and our hearts to the needs of the community we served each day. It shifted our hearts towards the heart of God, which always led back to His children.

While I was there, we also had our first Community Fall Festival. This allowed us to bring information and entertainment to West Dallas and just love on them for a whole day. We put action to our prayers and it was truly an amazing event. During this time, I began to realize that the call to school leadership expanded to borders beyond the school building itself and it reached into the homes and the land in which the school and those homes are built on.

I began to get a global perspective of this call. I realized with each regional assignment, God begins to birth a supernatural love for that place and the people who inhabit there. I had never been on a Missions trip, but I believe that West Dallas was my mission's assignment. Our school became a part of the local coalition of independent school district schools and we joined the fight for multi dwelling housing for our scholars' families that were being displaced because of slumlord housing violations.

Their burdens, needs, and cares became ours. And we

fought alongside the parents and the legislations for not just equality of education, but equality of life. Our hearts grew big and our reach grew farther. In each one of those assignments, God was able to show me that I not only was assigned to the school as its leader, but to the region—Southwest and West Dallas. My prayers began to increase from the teachers, to the scholars, to their parents, and their communities.

Let us pray that God begins to open our eyes to the region that our scholars are in and the needs of that territory. Let's pray a spirit of supernatural discernment would come upon us, as principals, that we may know the true hope of our calling and begin to decree that over our schools and the region they inhabit.

∽

Dear Omnipresent Father,

Thank You for the assignment You have given us as principals. We realize that You have seen this school, the students, and their families when they laid the foundation of the building. It is no accident where these schools are located and that You have appointed us to oversee the work at these schools.

Father, grant us the discernment to see what only You can see in the territory where these schools are located. Let us become sensitive to the news of the community and let us begin to legislate from heaven down to earth. Father, we decree and declare a hedge of protection around our schools that no hurt, harm, or danger may come near them. We commission angelic forces to encamp themselves around the city and state lines that no evil can even enter this territory. It has been conquered by the King of Kings and Lord of Lords.

Father, we are here to take back what the enemy has stolen. Father, as we walk in the power and authority You have given us, we bind drug addiction, sexual perversion, bullying, low self-esteem, poverty, and lack out of the region where our schools are. The enemy who has stolen in these areas will steal no longer. We will no longer live in fear of these areas taken over our schools and communities. We stand on Your Word, Lord, and cry out that Your presence infiltrate our communities, our cities, and our states in the Mighty Name of Jesus we pray. We that are watchmen on the wall of this school, see Your hand and Your face. We call to our city/states that the King of Glory is here. Bring all who are weary and worn and they will find the rest and peace that they need. Father, we decree that clarion call in every school, to every child, in every community across our nation. In Jesus' name, Amen.

THE SCHOOL – ELEMENTARY, MIDDLE, AND HIGH SCHOOL

He began to teach and say to them, "Is it not written, 'MY HOUSE SHALL BE CALLED A HOUSE OF PRAYER FOR ALL THE NATIONS'? But you have made it a ROBBERS' DEN."
Mark 11:17AMP

"There is a season (a time appointed) for everything and a time for every delight and event or purpose under heaven" Ecclesiastes 3:1 AMP

"The weapons of our warfare are not physical [weapons of flesh and blood]. Our weapons are divinely powerful for the destruction of fortresses." 2 Corinthians 10:4 AMP

"Therefore let us get past the elementary stage in the teachings about the Christ, advancing on to maturity and perfection and spiritual completeness, [doing this] without laying again a foundation of repentance from dead works and of faith toward God," Hebrews 6:1 AMP

Elementary School

"Simon, Simon, Satan has asked to sift all of you as wheat. But I have prayed for you, Simon, that your faith may not fail. And when you have turned back, strengthen your brothers." Luke 22:31-32 NIV

As a former primary principal, I have seen the enemy start to mess with the minds of our children at an alarmingly young age. We have students in pre-K being admitted to behavioral units because they were out of control or on ADHD medication that had them so doped up they could not actively participate in class. These are all distraction of the enemy to try and stop our children from discovering a love of learning and to truly become invested in themselves. At five and six years of age, they are spending less and less time in the educational environment and more time in the office or suspended due to their academic and/or behavioral gaps.

This will no longer happen at a school called by the Most High God. Being able to see heaven's perspective in earthly situations helps us to see the tactics and weapons that the enemy is forging against our students and say "No longer". Principals, this is where your position of authority and your prayer life must be aligned. The enemy has a strategic plan to destroy our future generations through the seeds that are planted in their lives at a young age. I had never seen so many cases of Kindergarten through second grade students so angry, overly exposed to violence and sex, depressed, and feeling hopeless...in Kindergarten! We can no longer stand around and watch this take place to our students.

Middle School

By the time a child has entered into the 2nd stage of educational maturation—middle school—he/she has not only developed social and emotional gaps but academic gaps as well. The enemy has sown seeds of anger, violence, and insecurity and now they are beginning to be a part of their personality. Middle school is the time when children began to push back on the rules that have been set for them.

They are no longer the young and impressionable Primary student, but now influencers, the leader of a clique, a bully, or an advocate for those who are being bullied. They are searching for their voice. They want to be seen by their peers and by you.

Principals, at this educational stage, we need to pray a hedge of protection around our student's identity. The enemy would like to present ideas and opportunities for a spirit of confusion to begin to set in. He knows that students at this age will begin to question authority and he uses that to drop in seeds of rebellion. We must protect our students through prayer during this crucial stage in their lives. We will continue to decree and declare that no weapon formed against them shall prosper. They will begin to know the Truth and the Truth will make them free.

High School

Once student have crossed over into high school, another influence becomes strong and now must be addressed in prayer—and these are friends. As a principal, you will begin to see the student in high school still looking for their identity, but now looking for someone or some group to identify with. This is another key way the enemy will execute his attack. During a time when students should be planning their future after high school and tapping into the gifts and talents that God has placed on their lives, their focus begins to shift to what the "world" is offering and what their "friends" are doing.

Each stage of education has challenges that our children have to face. They will not be able to face nor conquer these challenges without someone praying them through. Let's begin to decree God's promises over our children, so that His plans can succeed in every milestone of their education.

Dear Heavenly Father,

I pray over every age and stage that Your children go through during their educational journey. Lord. You said in Jeremiah 1:5, while you were in your mother' womb, I knew you and ordained you. So, I know that You have a perfect purpose and plan for each and every child. Lord, lead them by Your spirit to that perfect plan. During Elementary school, let Your voice be louder than any other voice speaking to them. Preserve their child-like faith in You and in the world. Isaiah 54:17 says, No weapon of anger, violence, depression, or ADHD that is formed against them will be able to prosper.

As they grow into Middle Schoolers, let them grow into the character and likeness of You. Let them see You when they look in the mirror and know that they are fearfully and wonderfully made as stated in Psalms 139:14. Lord, show them Your Love and Glory and let others see how uniquely set apart they are because of You.

Father, I know that high school is a huge turning point in a child's life. Surround them Lord, around the right people that will point them towards You. You know their hearts and what You have placed inside of them. Let that Light attract the divine connections and dispel those that would try to destroy that light. Lord, lead them to the hope and the future that You have for them.

May they receive Your best academically, emotionally, behaviorally, and socially, in Jesus' Name. Amen.

THE SCHOLL BUILDING

"This entire building is under construction and is continually growing under his supervision until it rises up completed as the holy temple of the Lord himself." Ephesians 2:21 TPT

I have had the privilege to be a part of two schools as they were being built. It was fascinating to watch the construction workers dig deep into the earth and pour the concrete to build a firm foundation for those schools. It is said that the higher you build a building, the deeper you have to dig for the foundation.

As I watched them pour the foundation, I could not help but to think about the students who would enter into the school buildings every day. We are pouring the foundation to their future through education. We are allowing them the opportunity to reach higher, dream bigger, and want more because they are within the school building.

As a principal, I felt that my only responsibility was to ensure that the building was a safe place for the students to come to each day, but I see now that my job was so much more. Covering the building in prayer allows God to enter into the building before the students and teachers come in. The Holy Spirit can begin to lay the foundation for the day and set the atmosphere for excellence.

When you are positioned in a place of power and authority, you can speak to the very ground that your school is built on and declare that each and every room in that building bring forth the students highest potential. Each doorway is an entry into what God has in store for their lives. We have a routine at our school that all teachers must be on "threshold" when students come into class and in the hallways during transition. This allows our presence to be seen and felt by all the students.

∼

Dear Heavenly Father,

We decree and declare that Your will is done in this building. That the very foundation would cry Holy and bow down and worship You, Father. When students enter into the building, let them feel Your love, peace, and safety. Father, every window and doorway welcomes students into Your presence. Father, I declare the foundation is built on to You. Where we are standing is truly Holy Ground. Let hallways sing Your praises and every doorway welcome your Spirit. Lord, we are so grateful to steward this school for Your glory. This building is not only an institution of learning, but Your sanctuary. You belong here and we honor You in this place. Father, bless this building and all who enter in it, in Jesus' Name. Amen.

OUR FAMILIES

⚜

"And in thee shall all families of the earth be blessed". Genesis 12:3b KJV

"We feel a personal responsibility to continually be thanking God for you, our spiritual family, every time we pray. And we have every reason to do so because your faith is growing marvelously beyond measure. The unselfish love each of you share for one another is increasing and overflowing." 2 Thessalonians 1:3 TPT

We know that without our families, we could not sustain the vision for high quality education and a safe, Godly environment for our children. It is important that our children have strong support systems to endure their educational journey, so we must pray and thank God for the families of our students. Let the Father's will be done in and outside of the school. May the love our students feel be an extension of the love and support they are receiving with their families.

Let us pray...

~

Dear Heavenly Father,

I come before You on behalf of all the families that are represented in our schools. Lord, we know how important the family unit is to You, so we ask that You strengthen our families in the Mighty Name of Jesus. Where there is division and dysfunction, Holy Spirit bring wholeness.

Let our families stand together in unity with our teachers and educators to build a firm foundation for our students. Father God, we speak strength. Strength to our fathers, whether present or absent, let them build a legacy of the importance of education as the building boxes towards their children's future. Let our fathers speak life into their children. A life with no limits nor boundaries to their lives and to their futures.

Let our mothers, whether present or absent, speak love into the hearts and minds of their children. Love will build their child's self-esteem, it will build their ability to have healthy friendships and relationships. Love lays the foundation for a generation to have compassion for their generation and the world.

Father, we bind the work of the enemy that would try to war against and destroy the family unit. Where there is unity, there is power.

Father, thank You for giving us the opportunity to not only lead students into Your presence, but their families, too. Every student in our building represents a family that needs You. Let the hope in their child's eyes and the love in their hearts be a testimony of Your power at work in their lives, and let every family give You all the glory, honor, and praise for the great things You have done.

Amen.

THE TEACHERS AND SUPPORT STAFF

"And [His gifts to the church were varied and] He Himself appointed some as apostles (special messengers, representatives), some as prophets (who speaks a new message from God to the people), some as evangelists (who spread the good news of salvation), and some as pastors and teachers (to shepherd and guide and instruct)." Ephesians 4:11 AMP

What an amazing gift to the Body of Christ and to our educational community. I don't think teachers understand how important their role is in the lives of the students that come in and out of their classrooms. The call is tremendous and the impact eternal.

Being called, as a principal, to cover our teachers and those who serve our students is a special call for me. I know how I felt in the classroom when I knew I needed someone to speak a word of encouragement to me in those rough days or lift up a silent prayer on the days when I was starting a new lesson and wanted to make sure that all my students understood the new material.

It's on those days when I needed a prayer covering the most. Someone who would go to the Lord on my behalf. Not just for the students that were before me, but for me. Praying that I would be the best teacher I could for them each and every day.

I remember in my third year of teaching, I had hit a wall in my student's progress. They were doing well on the network assessments and their growth was almost at a standstill. I remember going to my principal's office, closing her door, and saying, "I don't think I'm the right teacher for these kids. I'm not moving them in the way that they should be going, and I can't seem to find out how to consistently get them to show growth." I could feel the lump in my throat and the tears coming to my eyes, because the last thing I wanted to do was give up on my students. I just could not see a way out of my defeat. My principal sat there and she listened to me attentively and with a heart of compassion. She then handed me back my keys that I had put on her desk in the beginning of the confession and she said, "You are not going anywhere."

I started to argue back, and she said, "You are exactly who these scholars need. They are growing and changing as you are. The better you become at your skill and craft, the better they will become."

I said to her, "I don't want them to fail."

She said, "So, don't let them. What do you need to know and do to ensure that they won't fail?"

From that day on, we met once a week, went over my data, and looked for ways we could strengthen my content knowledge so that I was better equipped to teach them what they needed to know to succeed. I didn't give up because she wouldn't let me.

By the end of that year, my scholars had made double digit growth and were the top in the middle school and the second highest in the network. Pressing through that place of despair and discouragement caused my scholars to succeed, but I couldn't have done it without the support and encouragement of my principal.

She taught me to see myself the way that I saw my scholars—as winners. She pushed me and I pushed them over the finish line. At that moment, I knew I wanted to do for other teachers what she'd done for me.

∼

Dear Heavenly Father,

Father, I am so grateful for Your son, Jesus, who was the perfect Teacher. He taught the disciples in a way that they could learn. Never belittling them, but always preparing them to one day bring the gospel to others. It was by this method of 'differentiation' that we are all able to receive the Word of God and respond to His call upon our lives. But I do believe that many of those lessons were learned through the Holy Spirit, our paracletes, the one summoned, called to one's side, to one's aid. I am so thankful that You have given us those human forms through our teacher's aide and support staff. Without their continual support and willing hearts, our students and teachers would not be as successfully as they are. Father, let them know they are needed, appreciated, and loved by all that have the privileged to work with them each day. Cultivate their servant hearts that they may always praise You for the work they do for the Kingdom and our schools.

Bless them continually and in abundance. In Jesus' Name. Amen.

THE COMMUNITY

"Wise people are builders – they build families, businesses, communities. And through intelligence and insight their enterprises are established and endure." Proverbs 24:3 TPT

As a principal, I didn't realize how far my influence and impact reached. Thinking about it and the insigne of a pebble thrown into a pond, the ripples that the pebble makes is never ending.. Those ripples are like the prayers that are prayed over our teachers, our students, and their families. Their impact reaches far beyond the school, but into our neighborhoods and the communities we serve.

The community is the pavement in which students walk out the knowledge they received within the four walls of the schoolhouse. It is there where the true application of learning begins. Within International Baccalaureate, we are constantly trying to get our teachers to make "real world connections" through their lessons.

We often ask: *How can this lesson impact the world around you? And how can you take what you are learning and change your world?* For most of our students, those first seedlings show up in their community.

They begin to see their learning, not just as an escape from their current surroundings, but more as a way to change their surroundings and make it better. As they travel through each stage of educational development, they come to realize they are either part of the problem or part of the solution. Their communities then become the laboratory where innovation is developed and problems become opportunities to make their world, our world, a better place. Mahatma Gandhi said, "Be the change that you wish to see in the world."

So, with all of these responsibilities on our students to their community, what should they expect from the community? The community should be a place of love and support for our students as they grow and develop. There is a well-known proverb widely used within the African American community for generations that says, "It takes a village to raise a child."

I believe our communities are our modern day villages. There used to be a time, back in the day, when you got in trouble, you not only received discipline from your house, but you got a lecture from the neighbors, the people at the church, the store clerk at the corner store, the mailman, and the garbage collector. They were all your village. What they would nowadays call our "extended families".

∼

Father God,

Thank you for the communities You have place inside our schools. The place where unity lies and dreams are built by Your grace and love. Help us to steward these relationships with love, patience, and support. Let every member of our communities—staff, students, and their families—know how special and irreplaceable they are. Let them feel our prayers surrounding them in and outside of the school building. We are all one body in Christ and live to love one another as You love us. Thank You, Father, for reminding us that we need each other to make our communities strong and long lasting.

Thank You for teaching us to live together and love one another in unity.

You are an amazing Father.

Amen.

THE OPERATIONS

ATTENDANCE CLERK, REGISTRAR, FACILITIES, AND CAFETERIA WORKERS

"For God is not the author of confusion, but of peace, as in all churches of the saints." 1 Corinthians 14:33 KJV

When I think about what ultimately makes a school run smoothly, in order and peace, it's those hidden figures that we don't always see, but without them, we would feel their absence. As I began to meditate on those that need to be covered in prayer the most—before, during, and at the end of each day—it's the operations teams on the schools. They are the foundation that keeps the institution stable and running so that we can serve the teachers, students, and community as a whole.

At all of the schools where I have worked, I am usually the first one at the school and the last one to leave. The people that are usually there with me are the facility workers. They are putting up the cones for car lines, making the food for breakfast duty, checking all of the bathrooms to make sure there is enough toilet tissue and paper towels to last the day, and opening up the building to be able to welcome the families that will be coming in that morning.

They are always the first people at the school setting the tone of the day and making sure all is well before the day begins. When I would come in that early, I would find myself walking up each hallway, laying hands on lockers, classrooms, doors, and offices, but I never thought about those that were there with me in the wee hours of the morning. Those souls needed to be covered and prepared for all the day was going to bring them. The supplies that didn't come in, the workers that didn't show up, the students that come in late, and the parents that complain about... Everything!

It is those chosen people who come in everyday, prepared to take on the battles of the day with a greeting and a smile. I want to take the time to salute them. They are really the unsung heroes of each and every campus. I think of the receptionist that we just hired. She is truly a hidden warring angel. She reminds me of Michael, the Archangel. She is a sweet, soft spoken, young lady with a smile that lights up the front office, but a heart that is fearless against any attack that the enemy may bring her way. She always has a pleasant word to say to everyone, even the nastiest staff member or family member. I have never seen her be shaken, though I know that her armor takes may shots.

I know that I have been guilty some days to bark orders

at her or not greet her with the kindness she always greets me. And the amazing thing is, just like Jesus, she never treats me the way I have treated her. She smiles and shields all in the same matter, with no resentment or guile. I see the love of the Savior through her actions every day.

I would be remiss if I didn't pray over the facilities team. They truly give us a home away from home. What a servant's heart that is embodied in each of those young men and women as they walk the hallways, with a spirit champion and huge hearts. Their desire is to please the people they serve by picking up the trash every hour so that it never piles up in a teachers' classroom or bringing a lunch to a student who forgot it at home.

I know that at times it is difficult for them to serve under the stress and strain of others demands, but they are always willing and able to complete each request with dignity and grace. That servant spirit is setting them up for a greater glory in their lives. For they are willing to lay down everything for others, which makes them champions in my book. As a principal, I need these very vital individuals to be covered in prayer at all times, for they are the first line of defense before the school doors open and in the evenings when they close.

∼

Dear Heavenly Father, the author of peace.

Father be peace in these Your ambassadors of order and peace on our campuses this day. Father, You have assigned them specifi-

cally to each campus and school to fulfill the needs of their campus and their leaders and community.

Give them what they need to do their work in excellence that shows forth Your glory. Father, put Your words in their mouths as they interact with teachers, parents, and students. Let the words of their mouths and the meditations of their heart be acceptable in Your sight. Father, don't allow the arrows that form against them —by angry words from parents, teachers, leaders, neighbors in the community—penetrate their armor.

Father, keep their armor strong and intact for each battle they face every day. Father, let Your light shine bright through their faces, in their words, through their bodies, as they prepare the food in the café to the boxes that are delivered to classrooms. Let Your anointing go before them and strengthen them supernaturally.

Father, let them be keenly aware of Your presence walking in, through, and around them. For it is not by their might, not be their power, but by Your spirit that complete their daily tasks. As they seek You early in the morning, while they are driving to work or dropping their kids off at daycare or school, let them know that You have already been at the school and Your spirit has invaded each classroom they will clean, each tray they will fill with food, each closet they will stock with resources for the day. And Father, move on the hearts of those that they serve each day. Let our hearts be right to receive Your love through them. Let us treat them with the respect and dignity that their office requires.

Let us be quick to say 'hello' and 'thank you' and slow to bark orders and dismiss their efforts when they don't turn out the way we wanted it to. Father, we repent of our lack of kindness and *consideration to those You have brought in our lives to make the journey easier. We are sorry.* Change our minds so that we have Your mind and see them through Your eyes and love them with Your heart. Father, let us be aware of what we have not done to the least of them, we did not do to You. Keep this conviction in our hearts and as we serve those that You have sent to be of service to us. In Jesus' Name. Amen.

THE ORGANIZATION

"Don't bargain with God. Be direct. Ask for what you need. This isn't a cat-and-mouse, hide-and-seek game we're in. If your child asks for bread, do you trick him with sawdust? If he asks for fish, do you scare him with a live snake on his plate? As bad as you are, you wouldn't think of such a thing. You're at least decent to your own children. So don't you think the God who conceived you in love will be even better?" Matthew 7:7-11 MSG

Communities are just several families and extended family members living in the same location. The love and support that one community can give to one student can change the trajectory of the future of both parties. The umbrella that all of our schools stand under is the network/district.

Like our Father covers us, the network/district covers

our schools. It is the place that we get our funding from and our resources are funneled through. I find that as a principal, I am apart of both the campus vision as well as the network vision. It is the network vision that is manifested through each campus it covers. This is a place that every principal has to pray for discernment and spiritual eyes to see beyond the four walls of our schools.

There was a book that I lived by as a new principal titled "Leadership on the Line" by Ronald A. Heifetz and Marty Linsky. There is a concept that is called leading from the balcony and the dance floor. This was a very difficult concept for me to embrace because I had always been a leader on the dance floor, amongst my peers and within my campus.

As a principal, I had to ask myself the questions: How do I broaden my perspective to see leadership from the balcony? How do I see how my action and decisions impact the network and make a greater ripple in the sea of education?

I began to pray Ephesians 1:18-19 KJV: "The eyes of your understanding being enlightened; that ye may know what is the hope of his calling, and what the riches of the glory of his inheritance in the saints, And what is the exceeding greatness of his power to us-ward who believe, according to the working of his mighty power."

I believe this word manifesting in my life begin to reveal that "balcony" vision that I needed as a principal and allowed me to be able to pray from that perspective. I heard the Spirit of the Lord speaking about praying from heaven down. That's what kingdom dominion looks like. Speaking those things that are reveled on the balcony and praying them onto the dance floor of our schools.

Principals, I admonish you to take this stance as your influence and exposure increases. Let God magnify your visions so that you can see the hope to which He has called you to. It is that hope that the network/districts build their tenets on. It is the hope that education is the key that will unlock the future for our children. It is the hope that every student, in every classroom, in every school, can and will succeed. It is the hope that one great teacher can motivate the hearts of a thousand students and two great teachers can move 10,000 students. It is the hope that with every child that is convinced that knowledge is power and access is key, it will change the very trajectory of a family, of a community, of a nation. It is that hope that compels me to pray for the network/districts that support our schools to fulfill that hope.

The angels in the outfield, so to speak, are those school board members that stand in between the dance floor and the balcony advocating and interceding on behalf of our schools and how to best support them to be successful. As principals, we need to hold and support these people up in prayer. They have felt an inward call to volunteer and advocate for quality education for all students within our schools. Being a part of something greater changes a principal's whole posture in prayer. It's 'thy Kingdom come, thy will be done, on Earth as it is in Heaven.' Praying from the posture that this is a Father that wants the best for His children and if only we would ask, we will receive.

Let's begin to pray from this place, principals! That the provisions are there and we only need to ask the Father, and He will graciously give it to us, freely. Our networks and districts have all access to all that the Father has for them, we need only to ask Him.

∼

Dear Heavenly Father,

We declare that You are Jehovah Jireh, (our Provider). I know that You see ahead (from the balcony) and You provide (on the dance floor), so we are not afraid to ask of You all that we need to help our schools in the network/district. Father, we know that You see the needs that each of our school have. We trust that You will bring the needed supplies and resources in abundance for each school in their assigned district/network. Lord, we ask for Your favor to rest on each school so that grants will be fulfilled and bonds will multiply. At the end of the fiscal year, we are in the black and not in the red, in the name of Jesus.

Bless each network with employees filled with wisdom and understanding. Give them a heart to support their schools with compassion and grace. Anoint them with creative and innovative ideas and strategies to bring the needs, personnel, and resources into their districts and networks. We decree increase across our school districts/networks in the Mighty Name of Jesus.

Amen.

THE EDUCATIONAL SYSTEM

PUBLIC AND PRIVATE (MAKE US ONE)

"*B*ehold, how good and how pleasant it is for brethren to dwell together in **unity**!" Psalm 133:1 KJV

"Endeavouring to keep the **unity** of the Spirit in the bond of peace." Ephesians 4:3 KJV

"And if a kingdom be divided against itself, that kingdom cannot stand." Mark 3:24 KJV

In a system that is created to meet the needs of all mankind from infancy to adulthood, how did we become so divided? When did our different approaches cause a division instead of a unity? I'm not speaking about the people, as much as I'm speaking about the system.

How did the enemy get inside of the system and begin to corrupt the vision for education? The Lord's intent is for all to know the truth and that truth would make us free. The truth about who we are and who we will become is learned through the walls of education. That sacred institution broke the shackles of slavery and imprisonment for generations. We fought to learn and we learned to fight. What happened to that passion and desire to want access? To want more? There is power in a place of agreement. The enemy knows that and so he sows seeds of division between educational systems. God's plan is greater than any plan that the enemy could launch against the systems of this world. God knows there is power in the place of collective agreement and when we get together, our strength will complement our weaknesses and our students will all be successful. More than wanting to be "right" or wanting others to be "wrong", we want what is the best for our students, their families, and their communities. We want our students to have all the opportunities that a high quality education can open for them. God has placed so many gifts, talents, and abilities within our students, we have to create an environment where they can develop and grow. Our schools are a great place to begin that process. Diversity does not have to breed dissention, division, or discord. It can be a door with many different keys that unlock the brilliancy with our students. Let's work together and unlock every door.

Heavenly Father,

You said in Your word that it is a good thing for us to be in unity. Father, gives us unified hearts and minds. Let us desire one thing, that our students and their families receive all that education has for them, no matter what system it flows through. God, we know that You are in control and will bring us together so that Your will is done. Consecrate our hearts and renew a right spirit within us, so we accept each other in love. Unify Your body as one in Christ Jesus. Make us one Lord, Make us one.

Amen.

I believe every principal should have a "war room". A place to go and seek the Lord on behalf of the school they have been assigned to. God has so much He wants to say to you and give you divine strategies on how to steward this divine assignment.

My prayer is that you use this book as a guide as you pray to the Lord about your school. There are specific areas in each school that need God's covering. This book just highlights a few. Let the Lord speak to you through this book and ignite a fire for prayer over the schools.

Dear Heavenly Father,

Bless the school leader that has picked up this book and has prayed through it. Bless their school, staff, students, families, and communities. Let them know that You are there with them in every meeting and event. Your presence is in their building and Your guidance is only a prayer away. Strengthen and protect the vision You have placed inside of them and continue to cultivate love in their hearts. I am so grateful for them and their good fight of faith. May their school thrive and produce world changers and history makers.

In the Wonderful Name of Jesus.
Amen.

ABOUT THE AUTHOR

Suzanne Weathers is a woman with a heart for the Word and worship of God. She has been an educator for over 10 years, working as an assistant principal for two years and a principal for three years. She has a BA in Sociology with a minor in Education and a M.Ed with a specialization in Leadership in Urban Education. For the past 20 years, Suzanne has been involved in leadership in both music and prayer ministries in churches in New York and Texas. She has an online Facebook ministry called Diary of A Worshiper.

Suzanne is a joyful wife of her best friend, Michael, mother of three beautiful young girls, and a grandmother to a precious granddaughter. Including her newfound love for writing, she enjoys singing, reading, and watching movies with her family.

CPSIA information can be obtained
at www.ICGtesting.com
Printed in the USA
LVHW091412300919
632706LV00002B/530/P